Gemini

Astrology Zodiac Signs Coloring Book

The Horoscope Twins Sign (May 21 – June 21) Astrological Art For Adults & Teenagers

Rachel Mintz

Join Our Coloring Books VIP Group
Members Get Giveaways, Deep Discount Offers,
Win Prizes – Visit Site To Join (It's Free)

www.ColoringBookHome.com

GEMINI

GEMINI

GEMINI

GEMINI

GEMINI

Gemini

GEMINI

GEMINI

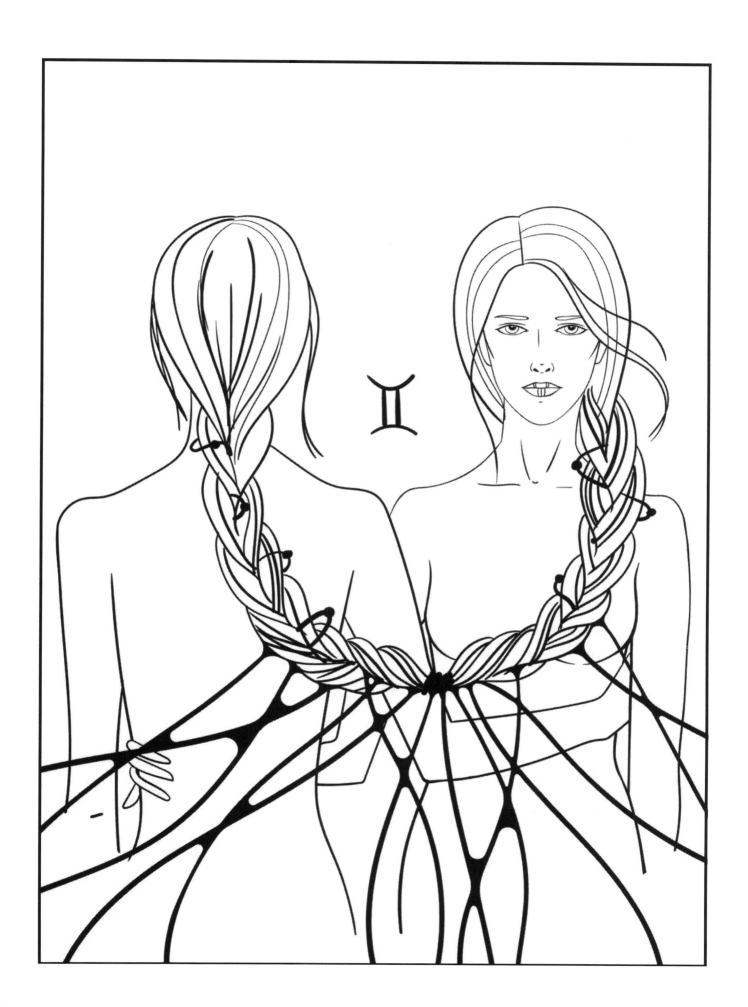

GEMINI

GEMINI

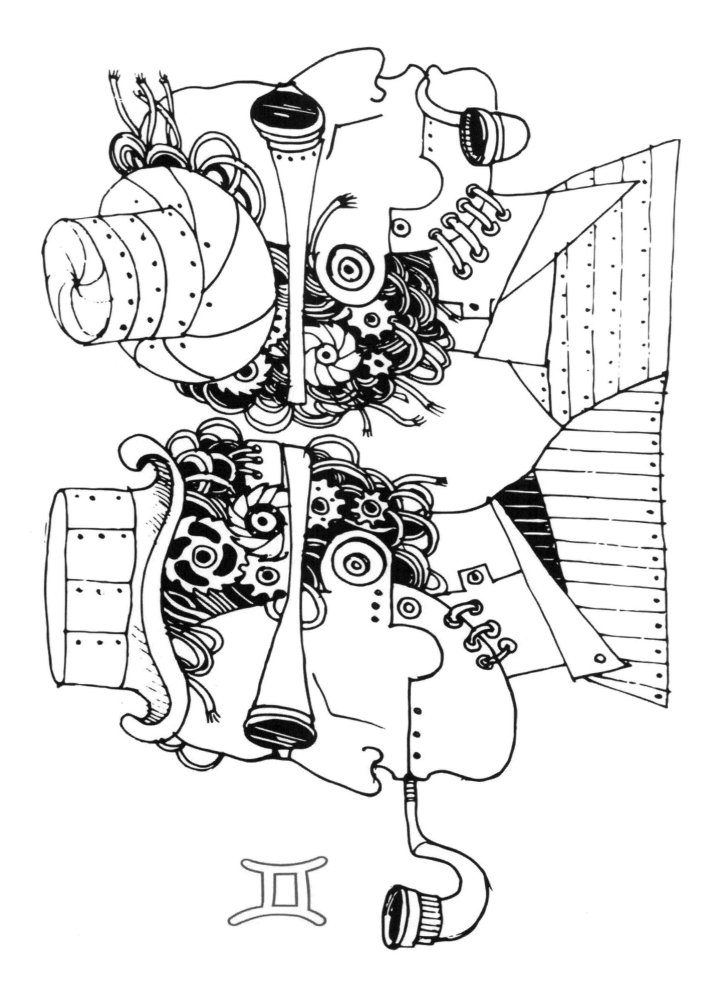

GEMINI

The 12 Zodiac Signs

Aries

Taurus

Gemini

Cancer

Leo

Virgo

Libra

Scorpio

Sagittarius

Capricorn

Aquarius

Pisces

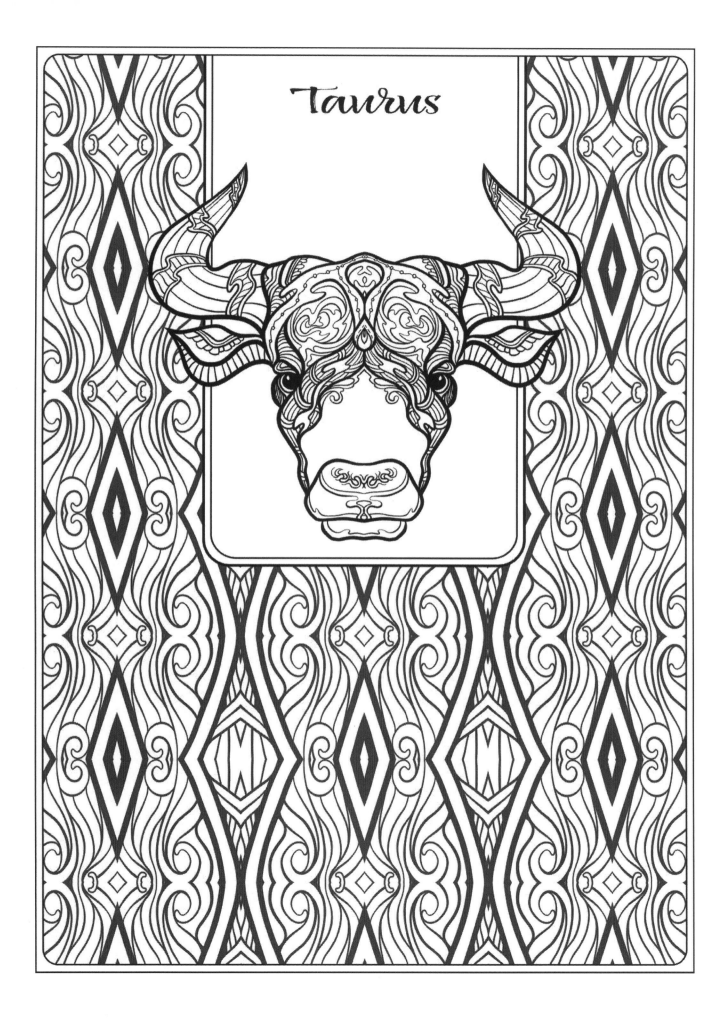

Taurus

Aries

Pisces

Scorpio

Thank you for coloring with us

Please rate & review

More RACHEL MINTZ Coloring Books For You at Amazon:

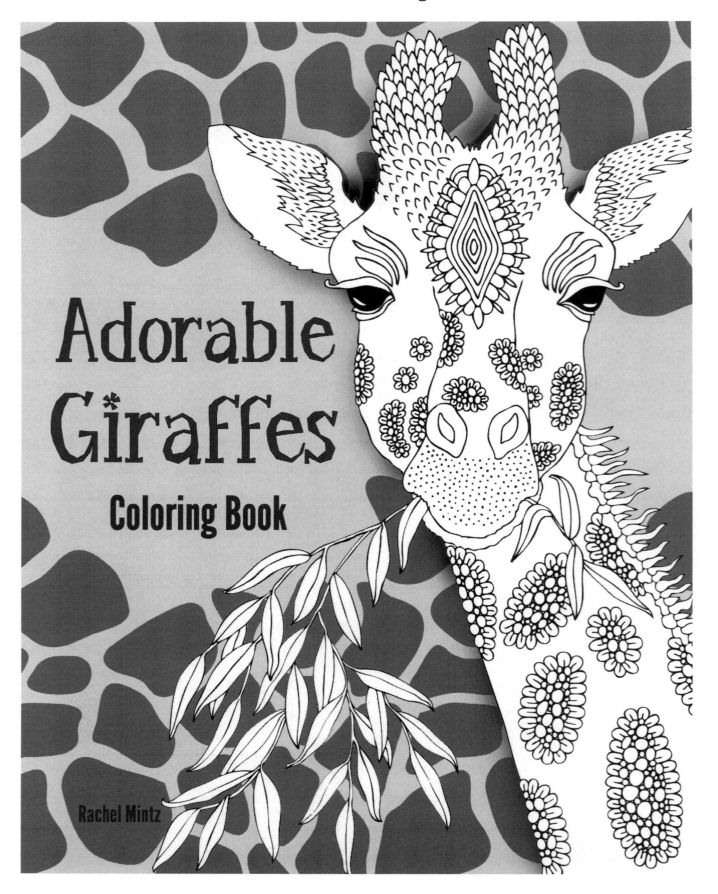

Adorable
Giraffes
Coloring Book

Rachel Mintz

My Coffee Break

Coloring Book

Rachel Mintz

Look for more RACHEL MINTZ coloring books at Amazon.

Mandalas | Wildlife | Marine Life| **Portraits** | Dogs | Cats | **Flowers** | Skulls | Gothic | Architecture | Romantic | Texts & Sayings | Ethnic | Steampunk | **Fashion** | Horses | Unicorns | Witches | Horror | Grayscale | Sports | Christmas | Holidays | Kids | Cars | **Motorbikes** | Trucks | Urban | Fairies | **Jewish Holidays**: Passover, Hanukkah, Purim | Safari | Pets |Multicultural | Educational for Kids | Back to School | **Preschool & Toddlers** | Army & Military | Knights & Castles | Dragons | Princesses | Butterflies | Birds | Reptiles | Bible | **Stained Glass** | Abstract | Machines | **Robots** | Space & Science | **Zombies** | Monsters | And many more topics..

Which topic do you like to color?

Search Amazon for 'Rachel Mintz + Your Topic' and find a book to color or as a gift.

Thank you for coloring with us

We will be very thankful if you could take the time to rate & review

Made in the USA
Middletown, DE
15 March 2023

26839933R00046